The Need for Cross-Domain Interoperability in a

Cyber Warfare Response:

Minimizing Threat Rigidity in

Emergency Management and Cyber Security

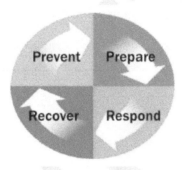

AUTHOR:

David G. Sweigert, M.Sci., CEH, CISA, CISSP, HCISSP, PMP, SEC+

Contents

Executive Summary

Civilized society -- and the emergency managers it relies upon to mitigate disasters -- can no longer ignore the potential for widespread "real-world" cyber warfare damage that can be inflicted upon the critical infrastructure which sustains basic life.

The cyber vulnerabilities of the nation's infrastructure are so widespread that experts often urgently cite the need for more cyber defenses and "fixes" without offering much in the way of practical recommendations to guide public response agencies on how to work around failed infrastructure.

The "doubling down" on the problem by deploying more costly defensive cyber equipment and fixes, which can be made moot in days as hackers work around such devices, is often times referred to as the "cyber security fallacy".

Focus can, and should, be placed on how public response agencies will deal with the downstream consequences of critical infrastructure failure in such an event. More interaction with cyber security practitioners by such agencies is needed.

As cyber security planners concentrate on familiar (and costly) "prevent and protect" strategies (fixes) they largely ignore unfamiliar strategies such as the need to overcome professional and cultural differences with emergency responders to improve a holistic "respond and recover" approach with public agency partners.

The author suggests that to improve cyber warfare defense resiliency more cohesive is needed between traditional emergency managers and cyber security experts. This is known as cross-domain interoperability.

Obstacles to achieving cross-domain interoperability may be the phenomena of "threat rigidity".

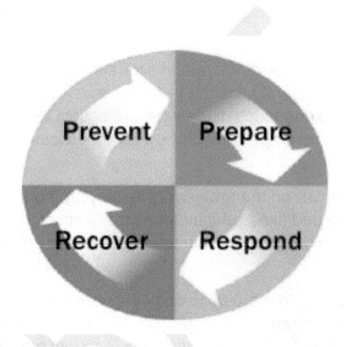

Research Paper Organization

The subject matter addressed in this paper is complex. The below format has been adopted to aid the reader in understanding this complex issue with a simplified document organization.

Highlighted key points are found in "Findings and Conclusions" section.

Data that has been analyzed that supports the Findings and Conclusions are presented in the section "Present State of Industry Activities".

References and end-notes are located in the ANNEX.

Findings and Conclusions

Important findings of this research

Present State of Industry Activities

Tutorial in nature, this section will document issues and the current state of affairs.

This section validates the findings and conclusions with supportive materials.

Annex

Cites

Findings and Conclusions

The Threat of Cyber Warfare

Adequate response strategies to wide-scale cyber-attacks are difficult to fashion. The complexity of inter-locking infrastructure can be daunting to planners. Nonetheless, this may be the Achilles heel of the United States.

A wide-scale surprise weaponized cyber-attack (an act of cyber warfare) will have a crippling effect on the United States.

As an example, a sophisticated cyber-attack could create widespread electrical power outages for weeks or even months. Attacks with similar consequences have already been prototyped in the Ukraine (massive power black-outs).

Malicious computer viruses (such as the WannaCry and Petya viruses out-breaks in the summer of 2017) shocked government officials and response agencies as the United Kingdom closed over sixty (60) hospitals while recovering from the damage inflicted to computer systems by such attacks.

Had the WannaCry or Petya viruses been effectively weaponized by cyber adversaries and used in a targeted fashion, damage to civilian infrastructure caused by downstream cascading infrastructure failures may have been profound.

Such pre-cyber warfare "mini-doomsday" scenarios have created public pressure on providers of critical infrastructure (electrical distribution, companies, waterways and dams, hospitals, airports, etc.) to develop adequate plans to address the potential for outages and loss of essential services.

When such weaponized cyber-attacks breach the security layer (or the invisible cyber fortress wall) the issue is no longer how to prevent such an attack, but how to respond to one.

The Private Ownership of Critical Infrastructure

The life-sustaining critical infrastructure of the United States represents a patch work of inter-dependent technology, organizations, and structures. If attacked at key vulnerable points, significant event failure sequences can amplify the catastrophic outcome and loss of essential services to the civilian population.

As the majority of critical infrastructure in the United States is owned by private owner/operators (some estimates are as are high as 85%), the responsibility for protection of such assets is distributed across a wide spectrum of private companies, cooperatives, quasi-private institutions, etc.

Wide-scale cyber warfare is an emerging threat that is unfamiliar to these infrastructure providers. The threat has largely been discussed in theoretical terms by public response and policy agencies.

Frustrating the goal of cyber infrastructure resiliency to such warfare is the avoidance of organizations to share information about their institution's cyber vulnerabilities, making the prediction of consequences by public response agencies and the identification of event failure sequences extremely challenging.

The situation described above represents disjointed and non-harmonized information sharing between two significant communities that will respond to a cyber warfare attack. This can be described as a lack of "cross-domain interoperability".

As defined by Wikipedia:

> **Cross-domain interoperability** *exists when organizations or systems from different domains interact in* <u>information exchange</u>, *services, and/or goods to achieve their own or common goals.* <u>Interoperability</u> *is the method of systems working together (inter-operate). A domain in this instance is a community with its related infrastructure, bound by common purpose and interests, with consistent mutual interactions or rules of engagement that is separable from other communities by social, technical, linguistic, professional, legal or sovereignty related boundaries*

The Threat Rigidity Phenomena

Radical new unfamiliar threats – like cyber warfare – can exacerbate the problem on non-interoperability. One theory states that as the awareness of the threat grows, the response to such an unfamiliar threat tends to exhibit cognitive narrowing and over-simplification by responders.

This phenomena is known generally as "Threat Rigidity". Researchers have likened the phenomena to a doubling down of familiar approaches when confronted by a new threat. In the protect/prevent methodology this would be increased cyber devices and fixes to prevent a penetration of the cyber fortress wall. In the respond/recover methodology this may mean an increase in situational awareness reporting or status reporting (without any accompanying mitigation activity).

Maladaptive and disjointed cyber warfare response strategies may only intensify the threat. For example, high impact / low probability threats (such as cyber warfare) represent an emergent threat that does not easily fit into familiar predetermined risk categories and may be glossed over (over-simplified) by emergency response planners.

Such outcomes would be maladaptive response (threat rigidity) such as what is popularly known as the "ostrich sticking its head in the sand" – which is ignoring the threat altogether.

Titanic Disaster

The Titanic disaster may offer an example of threat rigidity on the part of the crew (response agencies). The new threat (striking ice berg) was addressed by a doubling down of traditional responses ("man the life boats"). However, other innovative strategies (such as placing passengers on the ice berg itself to await rescue) were not considered.

Conclusions

- A well-coordinated successful cyber-attack could inflict grave real-world damage to the nation's critical infrastructure sectors.

- The community of public response agencies should increase communications and contact with cyber security practitioners, with the end goal to interface both into an overall cyber-centric disaster response and enhance cross-domain interoperability.

- Communicating the complexity of cyber-attacks, when viewed in the context of traditional natural disasters that tend to have a historically predictable outcome, can be frustrated by culturally differences between the two domains.

- Increasing cross-domain interoperability between these professions (domains) is sorely needed to adequately prepare for a "not if, but when" wide-scale cyber-attack on critical infrastructure.

- Culturally differences in the two professions relied on most in this area (emergency management and cyber security) are preventing cohesive approach to the problem.

- Unified and blended training and exercise preparations need to become a national priority to bring awareness to the need for cross-industry interoperability.

Present State of Industry Activities

As defined by the United Nations, critical infrastructure is:

The physical structures, facilities, networks and other assets which provide services that are essential to the social and economic functioning of a community or society.[i]

U.S. Government view of protecting Critical Infrastructure

Privately owned critical infrastructure (C.I.) owners/operators are responsible for the protection of more than percent of the 85% of the nation's C.I.[ii] . Private resources and assets are inextricably intertwined into a fabric that supports that operations of business, academia, government and daily life. These cyber-centric resources are under constant attack by a host of cyber adversaries.

The U.S. Department of Homeland Security (DHS) classifies this C.I. in sectors.

These sectors include:

Critical Infrastructure Sectors	
Chemical	Commercial Facilities
Communications	Critical manufacturing
Dams	Defense Industrial Base
Emergency Services	Energy
Financial services	Food and Agriculture
Government Facilities	Healthcare and Public Health
Information technology	Water and Wastewater Systems
Transportation Systems	Nuclear Reactors, Materials

Examples of critical infrastructure[iii]

The national protection approach to these C.I. industry "sectors" is defined by Presidential Policy Directive 21, entitled: "Critical Infrastructure Security and Resilience", issued 2/12/2013[iv].

Each sector has a Sector Specific Agency (SSA) that coordinates the protection for that sector. These SSAs can provide a moderating role in providing guidance to C.I. operators with regards to the emergency management circle.

Overall protection planning is coordinated by the U.S. Department of Homeland Security (DHS), National Protection and Programs Directorate (NIPD)[v].

For example, the U.S. Department of Energy produced the *"Energy Sector-Specific Plan" (SSP)* in 2015[vi] with the U.S. Department of Homeland Security (DHS) quoting in relevant part:

> *The 2015 Energy Sector-Specific Plan (SSP) was developed in accordance with the NIPP 2013: Partnering for Critical Infrastructure Security and Resilience, which guides the national effort to manage risk to the Nation's critical infrastructure.*

> *The 2015 Energy SSP updates and augments the prior versions of the SSP in accordance with the NIPP 2013. Specifically, it includes the discussion of the many evolving risks and threats in the Energy Sector, as well as an increased emphasis on the Energy- and cross-sector interdependency issues and the integration of cyber and physical security efforts.*

Table 2-1: National and Energy Sector Critical Infrastructure Vision and Goals

VISION STATEMENT
A Nation in which physical and cyber critical infrastructure remain secure and resilient, with vulnerabilities reduced, consequences minimized, threats identified and disrupted, and response and recovery hastened.
From the 2015 SSP

Understanding the Emergency Management profession

Emergency Managers (E.M.s) are professionals that have been trained to manage conditions in a disaster or catastrophic situation. Often times the public thinks of the Federal Emergency Management Administration (FEMA) as comprised of emergency managers.

Emergency management is sometimes referred to as: disaster management, crisis management, or activities undertaken to recover from a catastrophic event, etc.

It is instructive to note the United Nations definition of a disaster:

> *A serious disruption of the functioning of a community or a society at any scale due to hazardous events interacting with conditions of exposure, vulnerability and capacity, leading to one or more of the following: human, material, economic and environmental losses and impacts.*[vii]

Generally, E.M.'s are not charged with protecting or preventing attacks to C.I. as infrastructure does not necessarily impact a community until it fails. When the failure "event" occurs, the job of the E.M. is to coordinate the response activities to: (1) protect lives and reduce injuries, (2) reduce damage property, (3) help to community move on to a "new normal", or return back to normal life.

In essence, E.M.s address "real-world" problems, disasters that manifest in the physical world. It may be challenging for such individuals to comprehend the intangible area of "cyber space" and the potential for real-word consequences. Familiar to emergency managers are events such as failures of C.I.; such:

- Hazardous Material chemical spills/releases
- Train Derailments/chemical spills
- Wildland Fires/evacuation orders/sheltering populations
- Dam Compromise/evacuation/sheltering of populations

The capstone industry certification for the E.M. community is the Certified Emergency Manager (CEM) designation issued by the International Association of Emergency Managers (IAEM).

A useful snapshot of the industry was provided by Margaret Steen in her article "*Professionals Debate the Need for Emergency management Certification*"viii, quoting in relevant part:

> *The CEM certification came from a sense in the early '90s that the profession needed to become more sophisticated, said Dean R. Larson, president of Larson Performance Consulting in Munster, Ind., and chair of the USA CEM Commission for the International Association of Emergency Managers (IAEM).*
>
> *Emergency management's "roots came from civil defense," said Larson. "As civil defense started to become broader than just preparing for a response to enemy attacks, there was a need for a significant upgrade in emergency management."*
>
> *The evolution of strategies — such as the <u>all-hazards approach</u>, which used a similar structure for all disasters, whether natural or man-made, accidental or intentional — highlighted the need for more professional managers, Larson said. The IAEM created a standard body of knowledge for emergency managers, then set requirements for them to meet to become certified.*

A recent public government agency vacancy announcement for an "Emergency Manager" provides insight into the required "Knowledge, Skills and Abilities" (KSAs)ix.

> *Knowledge of:*
>
> - *Emergency Management principles, methods and techniques.*
> - *Practices and principles of public administration and government fiscal management, including budget preparation, expenditure control, contract administration, and recordkeeping.*
> - *Applicable Federal (including FEMA), State and local laws, rules, regulations and policies.*
> - *State-of-the-art community emergency preparedness programs.*
> - *Governmental structure and functions during emergency situations.*
> - *Community resources available to emergency management.*
> - *Volunteer management and administration practices*
> - *Emergency Operations Centers activation to include processes, direction and control and situational assessments*
> - *Grant writing and application process, as well as accounting principles used in grant accounting.*

The partial job requirements shown above is representative of the industry and demonstrates that E.M.s (e.g. CEMs) are assumed to have a wide background and skill sets in community relations, problem solving, emergency operations, volunteer management, obtaining grant monies, etc. To generalize – response and recovery skills.

E.M.s rely on the foundational "activity wheel" to describe their approach to potential threats that result in actual disasters/emergencies. Caveat: this foundational wheel was also included in the job description referenced above.

The Four Phases of Emergency Management	
Mitigation: Preventing future emergencies or minimizing their effects. Before and after an event. Efforts to identify risks and reduce them.	Response: Responding safely to an emergency. During and after the event.
Preparedness: Preparing to handle an emergency. Before the event.	Recovery: Recovering from an emergency. After an event. Returning to a "new normal".

Emergency Management challenges in preparing for the cyber war

The significance of widespread cyber-attacks (cyber warfare) disrupting infrastructure with physical real-world consequences hasn't been widely discussed in the E.M. industry. In fact, many well-intentioned institutions are seemingly trying to play "catch-up" with the publication of new awareness campaigns by government agencies and regulators.

As an example, the Joint Commission (an accreditation body familiar to every major hospital and healthcare delivery organization) recently published the web-page "Emergency Management Resources – Cyber Attack", 5/17/2017[x] (see below).

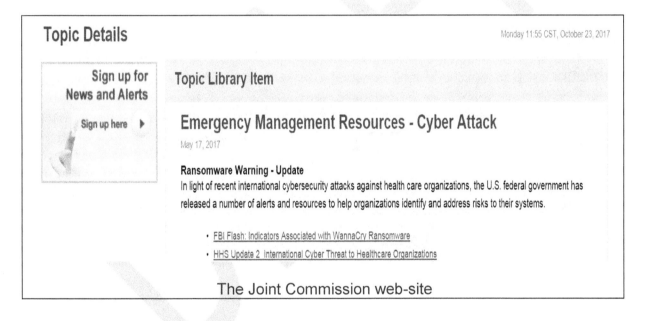

The Joint Commission ("Commission") response (above) followed the WannaCry computer virus outbreak in May 2017. The Commission was justifiable concerned as the WannaCry virus outbreak was attributed as directly responsible for the closure sixty (60) hospitals in the United Kingdom.

Example of emergency managers in an
Emergency Operations Center[xi]

E.M.s are not necessarily specifically focused on the consequences of a cyber warfare event, or for that matter, cyber security in general. To illustrate there are no vendors with a cyber or computer security orientation exhibiting at this year's IAEM Annual Conference; EMEX 17.

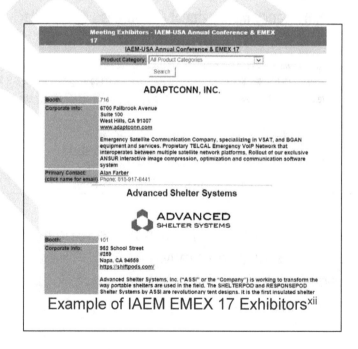

Example of IAEM EMEX 17 Exhibitors[xii]

The types of products and services showcased at EMEX 17 follow familiar lines with the specific vocabulary and jargon used within the industry. Examples include:

> *Business Continuity Planning Asia Pte Ltd (BCP Asia) is the leading provider of training and consultancy in **Business Continuity Management (BCM), Emergency Management, Crisis Management, Disaster Recovery and Enterprise Risk Management (ERM)***

> BOLDplanning focuses exclusively on **Continuity of Operations Planning, Continuity of Government (COG), Emergency Operations Planning (EOP), and Hazard Mitigation Planning (HMP)** for government emergency managers.

Such specific jargon may not be used by private C.I. owners and operators. There are differences in documentation titles between the public-centric E.M. community and private cyber security practitioners.

Private industry cyber security practitioners rely on documents such as: Business Continuity Plan, Disaster Response Plan, Emergency Mode of Operations Plan, Business Impact Analysis, etc.

The situation described above represents disjointed and non-harmonized vocabulary between two significant communities that will response to a cyber warfare attack. This is known as a lack of "cross-domain interoperability".

As defined by Wikipedia:

> ***Cross-domain interoperability*** *exists when organizations or systems from different domains interact in* <u>*information exchange*</u>*, services, and/or goods to achieve their own or common goals.* <u>*Interoperability*</u> *is the method of systems working together (inter-operate). A domain in this instance is a community with its related infrastructure, bound by common purpose and interests, with consistent mutual interactions or rules of engagement that is separable from other communities by social, technical, linguistic, professional, legal or sovereignty related boundaries*

Understanding the impact of Threat Rigidity and non-Cross Domain Interoperability

Traditionally, emergency managers have relied on highly predictable and familiar risk models of disasters and their outcomes (usually natural disasters, e.g.: multi-county floods, 10,000 acre wildland fires, multi-state hurricane land fall, etc.).

The impacts caused by cyber warfare will not necessarily follow the traditional risk models conceived for natural disasters. In fact, if such an attack is intelligently executed by motivated attackers, that exploit cascading damage caused by interdependencies, damage is expected to far exceed traditional natural disasters.

The above described situation is a fertile environment for the growth of "Threat Rigidity", a term coined by researchers Staw, Sandelands and Dutton in 1981. Quoting from "The Threat Rigidity Effect":

> **Meaning:** *When under threat or in crisis, companies are inclined to more firmly focus on the one thing they do well (e.g. their core product or service), stop doing other things, and become more hierarchical and top-down in terms of management control. The term was first used in organisational behaviour theory by Barry M Staw of the University of California at Berkley.[xiii]*

Threat Rigidity can be discussed within the context of radical new threats, which require flexible approaches to address them. However, cognitive over-simplification by response personnel can lead to the development of maladaptive approaches. This concept was addressed in the SANS Institute whitepaper "Threat Rigidity in Cybersecurity"; quoting author Michael Weeks[xiv]:

> *Highly visible cybersecurity events likely have the effect of moving organizations into a Threat Rigidity state.*

To summarize, Threat Rigidity is much like the Fight – Flight – Freeze response characteristics displayed by humans when facing new threats. Many camera videos of armed robberies at bank ATM devices reveal bank consumers "frozen in fear" when a gun is thrust upon them by the robber.

Unfamiliar with the situation the tendency is to "shut down", "withdraw" or freeze.

In the book, *Information Systems for Emergency Management*, authors Van De Walle, Turoff and Hiltz[xv] combine "Threat Rigidity" with the concept of "Groupthink" (the idea of majority opinion stifling minority opinions, even if the minority is correct).

> *Groupthink may be the result may be the result of any number of causes. For example, peer pressure can have a powerful effect on individuals. Even without overt pressure, an individual who experiences feelings of uncertainty, especially in complex, ambiguous situations, may defer to the consensus of the majority in what has been called "the majority effect" or "Asch effect".*

Defending the cyber castle

Many cyber researchers have concluded that strengthening the enterprise is a fallacy much like strengthen medieval castles in Europe. The era of enterprise hardening and "cyber castle defending" has fostered an environment where creative hackers and malicious cyber adversaries can circumvent counter-measures almost on the very day these protect/prevent devices are deployed.

Author Jamie Madison points out, in her article "*Dealing with the Biggest Cybersecurity Fallacy in the Enterprise*", the following:

> *Here's the thing – in 2013, a joint study by Ponemon and Symantec found that most data breaches that year were actually the result of human error.*

> *What a lot of people seemed to forget was that the security threats facing any given organization were not entirely external – nor were they all digital. Physical loss or theft, malicious insiders, employee ignorance, and lax security standards are all threats that generally have no bearing on whether or not the information's encrypted.[xvi]*

In his article "*Why America's Current Approach to Cybersecurity Is So Dangerous*", Gregory Michaelids opines[xvii]:

Right now, America's collective cybersecurity effort is headed toward near-certain failure for reasons within our own control. In less than a decade—thanks to the influx of dollars and high-level policy and press attention—cybersecurity has transformed what is actually a "people problem with a technology component" into its exact opposite. It's not too late to change course. But that first requires rejecting the fallacy that individuals can, or should, simply wait around to be passive recipients of cybersecurity.

But when we shift from talking about the problem of cybersecurity to the solution, it's clear we've drifted dangerously off a sensible course. Official Washington and Silicon Valley have adopted a set of faulty assumptions about cybersecurity and internalized them to such a degree it's practically a new religion, somewhere between late–19th century technological determinism and medieval alchemy. The core tenet of this mistaken faith? It fits on a single tablet: that cybersecurity will magically emerge once the right mixture of technology, regulation, and market incentives are poured into the cauldron. Ordinary people need not apply.

There's no "cyber–CDC."

The above words are amplified by a cyber security expert with 30 years of experience, Jerry Hutcheson, who published a LinkedIn article entitles, "The IT Security Fallacy"[xviii], stating:

For all of these years, there have been technology upgrades developments and promises about security technology. The claims were just as big and bold. If you don't use this new appliance or that new software you will be doomed to suffer a security attack of major proportions and will be destroyed.

The estimate of total cost of cyber attacks in 2014 was estimated by a McCaffe study at around $445 billion. And it has gone up every year. And estimates say that it could reach as high as $6 trillion by the year 2021. Whatever we are doing is not working very well.

The constant search for that magic technology pill that is going to save us is not only ineffective, it is harmful. It takes our eye off of the ball. We lose sight of the goal. I have quoted Vince Lombardi before on this he said, "an obstacle is what you are looking at when you take your eye off the goal." Don't take your eye off the goal.

ANNEX A

Cites and Sources

Website addressing Hospital Incident Command System

http://www.emsa.ca.gov/disaster_medical_services_division_hospital_incident_comman
d_system_resources

White paper by author:

https://www.slideshare.net/dgsweigert/nursing-meets-hacking-medical-computer-
emergency-response-teams-medcert

Nursing meets Hacking -- Medical Computer Emergency Response Teams –
MedCERT, June 7, 2017

White paper by author:

https://www.slideshare.net/dgsweigert/the-cyber-first-responder-and-the-hospital-
incident-command-system-75824159

The Cyber First Responder and the Hospital Incident Command System, May 9, 2017

White paper by author:

https://www.slideshare.net/dgsweigert/post-wannacry-hospital-cybersecurity-needs-to-
link-to-emergency-management

Post WannaCry: Hospital cybersecurity needs to link to Emergency Management, May
19, 2017

i https://www.unisdr.org/we/inform/terminology

ii http://www.hlswatch.com/2009/03/16/85-percent-is-wrong/

iii https://emilms.fema.gov/IS921/images/splash_03.jpg

iv https://obamawhitehouse.archives.gov/the-press-office/2013/02/12/presidential-policy-directive-critical-infrastructure-security-and-resil

v https://www.dhs.gov/national-protection-and-programs-directorate

vi https://www.dhs.gov/sites/default/files/publications/nipp-ssp-energy-2015-508.pdf

vii https://www.unisdr.org/we/inform/terminology

viii http://www.govtech.com/em/training/Professionals-Debate-Emergency-Management-Certification.html

ix
http://agency.governmentjobs.com/kitsap/job_bulletin.cfm?jobID=1852028&sharedWindow=0

x http://www.jointcommission.org/emergency_management_resources_cyber_attack/

xi
https://sfdem.files.wordpress.com/2012/03/5612_94693154229_60874484229_2046419_720947_n.jpg

xii
https://members.iaem.com/members_online/registration/exhdirectory.asp?mt=AC17&af=IAEM

xiii https://economictimes.indiatimes.com/magazines/corporate-dossier/buzz-word-threat-rigidity-effect/articleshow/4704294.cms

xiv https://www.sans.org/reading-room/whitepapers/critical/threat-rigidity-cybersecurity-38135

xv

https://books.google.com/books?id=DknfBQAAQBAJ&pg=PA65&lpg=PA65&dq=threat+rigidity+in+emergency+management&source=bl&ots=fiyPVWGsuG&sig=De6kGy5QzYPvbIHQ5qvE1MDSL28&hl=en&sa=X&ved=0ahUKEwiLrqmUo63XAhUB3WMKHdyDD6IQ6AEIPzAC#v=onepage&q=threat%20rigidity%20in%20emergency%20management&f=false

xvi https://blog.semaphore-software.com/cybersecurity-fallacy-in-enterprise.html

xvii

http://www.slate.com/articles/technology/future_tense/2017/03/why_america_s_current_approach_to_cybersecurity_is_so_dangerous.html

xviii https://www.linkedin.com/pulse/security-fallacy-jerry-hutcheson

www.ingramcontent.com/pod-product-compliance
Lightning Source LLC
Chambersburg PA
CBHW082132070326

40690CB00050B/4363